Big Bang
SCIENCE EXPERIMENTS

IT's ALIVE!

THE SCIENCE OF PLANTS AND LIVING THINGS

Jay Hawkins

WINDMILL BOOKS

New York

Published in 2013 by Windmill Books, An Imprint of Rosen Publishing
29 East 21st Street, New York, NY 10010

First Edition

Editors: Joe Harris and Samantha Noonan
Illustrations: Andrew Painter
Step-by-Step Photography: Sally Henry and Trevor Cook
Science Consultant: Sean Connolly
Layout Design: Orwell Design

Picture Credits:
Cover: JLP/Jose L. Pelaez/Corbis
Interiors: Photo Researchers/FLPA 4–5. Shutterstock: 13br (Thomas M. Perkins).

Library of Congress Cataloging-in-Publication Data

Hawkins, Jay.
 It's alive! : the science of plants and living things / by Jay Hawkins.
    p. cm. — (Big bang science experiments)
 Includes index.
 ISBN 978-1-4777-0322-9 (library binding) — ISBN 978-1-4777-0365-6 (pbk.) —
 ISBN 978-1-4777-0366-3 (6-pack)
 1. Biology—Experiments—Juvenile literature. I. Title.
 QH316.5.H39 2013
 570.72'4--dc23
                                        2012026225

Printed in China

CPSIA Compliance Information: Batch #AW3102WM: For Further Information contact Windmill Books, New York, New York at 1-866-478-0556
SL002560US

CONTENTS

This book is a matter of life and death!

BEE BOP

Did you know that honeybees can communicate by dancing? Their "waggle dances" can tell other members of the hive where to find pollen-rich flowers! This book is packed with experiments and facts exploring the science of living things.

THE JITTERBUG

When a bee has found a good source of food, she dances for other bees in the hive. First, she walks forward in a straight line, excitedly waggling her body. Then she walks back to where she started in a figure-eight pattern.

SUPERBUGS!

Bees are very important to us. When they travel between flowers, collecting nectar, they carry pollen from one flower to the next. This pollen enables flowers to turn into fruits. Without the bees' waggle dance, we wouldn't have any fruit!

WAGGLE WORDS

How do bees make sense of a waggle dance? The direction of the dance tells them about the angle between the Sun and the new source of food. The length of the dance tells them how far away the food is.

BENDING A CHICKEN BONE

Everybody knows that bones are hard. Or are they? Freak out your family and friends by turning a chicken bone soft and rubbery.

YOU WILL NEED:

★ A large clean jar with a lid

★ A chicken bone, a "drumstick" works best

★ Vinegar

Step 1

Save the bone from a drumstick after a chicken meal.

Step 2

Remove any meat from the bone and rinse it under running water.

What a great excuse for a barbecue!

Step 3

Notice how hard and stiff the bone is. Bones contain a mineral called calcium to make them hard.

Step 4

Put the bone in the jar, then pour vinegar in so it covers the bone completely.

Now you have to wait for the "magic" to happen ...

Step 5

After four days, open the jar and take out the bone. Rinse it with water and see how bendy it is! Pour the vinegar away down the sink.

HOW DOES IT WORK?

The vinegar dissolves the calcium in the bone. The calcium is what made the bone strong and hard and without it, the bone becomes soft and bendable. This is why it's important for you to get enough calcium in your diet—trying to walk around with bendy bones wouldn't be very fun!

SILLY CELERY

Have you ever seen a plant with blue leaves? Here's how you can dye plants different colors.

YOU WILL NEED:

★ Sticks of celery with leaves still on

★ 2 small glasses

★ 2 bottles of food coloring

★ Water

★ A work top or table

★ Kitchen scissors

Does a celery seller earn a good salary?

Step 1

Pour water into a glass so it is a third full. Add three drops of food coloring.

Step 2

Trim the bottom of a stick of celery so that it is about 6 inches (15 cm) long. Leave the leaves on.

Step 3

Put the end of the celery into the liquid in the glass. Leave the glass in a safe place, where it won't be moved.

Step 4

Ater one day, cut across the base of the celery with scissorts. You will see lines of color rising up the stalk.

Step 5

Split another stick of celery. Put colored water in two glasses. Allow each part of the split stalk to stand in a glass.

Step 6

The following day you will have multicolored celery! Cut back the stalks to check.

HOW DOES IT WORK?

Plants take up water from the soil through their roots. The water travels all the way up the stems to the leaves, through tubes called the xylem. If you put dye in the water, then that will be taken up too. Try the experiment with a white flower to see the petals change color!

HOW BIG ARE YOUR LUNGS?

I'll huff and I'll puff and I'll...test my lung capacity! Try out this simple experiment to see exactly how much air your lungs can hold.

YOU WILL NEED:

★ An empty 2 liter soda bottle
★ A medium-sized bowl
★ A big bowl
★ A bendy straw
★ Water
★ Lots of puff!

Step 1

Fill a bottle with water right to the top.

Step 2

Screw the cap on.

It is possible to increase your lung capacity with practice.

Step 3

Put the smaller bowl in the bigger bowl. Add water to the smaller bowl until it is ¾ full.

Step 4

Hold the bottle in the bowl with the neck in the water and take off the cap.

Step 5

Take a deep breath!

Step 6

Put the end of the straw in the bottle and blow out one big breath!

Keep the neck of the bottle under the water!

Step 7

You will be able to see how much air you can store in your lungs! Ask a friend or family member to try the experiment. Who has the biggest lung capacity?

HOW DOES IT WORK?

When you blow down, the air you breath out displaces the water that was in the bottle. The empty space is exactly equal to how much air your lungs can hold.

YEAST BALLOON

Yeast is a tiny microorganism that has a massive impact on your life. See the amazing power of yeast by using it to blow up a balloon.

YOU WILL NEED:

★ Warm water

★ A packet of dry active yeast

★ A spoon

★ A pitcher

★ Sugar

★ A small plastic soda bottle

★ A balloon

Step 1

Pour 10 fl. oz. (300 ml) of water into a bowl. Add a packet of dry yeast and 2 tablespoons of sugar and stir the mixture until the yeast and sugar have dissolved.

Step 2

Pour the mixture into the drinks bottle.

Step 3

Warm up the balloon in your hands. To soften the rubber more, grip the ends of the balloon and stretch it.

Will your yeast "rise" to the challenge?

Stretch the open end of the balloon over the neck of the bottle. Make sure it is pulled down over the screw threads on the top of the bottle to prevent air from leaking.

Step 5

Leave the bottle upright with the balloon fitted for one hour, then check the result!

Step 6

Leave the bottle undisturbed overnight. In the morning the balloon will be even bigger!

HOW DOES IT WORK?

The yeast needs sugar and water to activate it and it begins to respire (breathe). As it does this, it creates the gas carbon dioxide, which is what blows up the balloon. Yeast is what we use to make bread rise, so it is a very important little creature!

FOOD ON THE FLY

Attention all animal lovers! These ingenious bird feeders will attract birds and squirrels to your garden. Then you can observe them and learn all about them!

BOTTLE BIRD FEEDER

YOU WILL NEED:

* ★ A 2-liter plastic soda bottle
* ★ Plastic milk or yogurt containers
* ★ String
* ★ Birdseed
* ★ Scissors

Step 1

Ask an adult to help you cut a circular hole about 2 inches (5 cm) across in the side of a 2-liter soda bottle, using scissors.

Sometimes squirrels will also eat birdseed.

Step 2

Tie some string around the top of the bottle.

Step 3

Pour some birdseed into your bottle. The seed should nearly reach the hole when the bottle stands upright.

Step 4

Hang up your bird feeder bottle outside where the birds can feed safely. It needs to be high, so they won't feel threatened by cats and other predators.

PEANUT CONES AND POPCORN TREATS

YOU WILL NEED:

★ A pinecone
★ String
★ Peanut butter
★ A spoon
★ Birdseed
★ Popcorn
★ Needle and thread

That doesn't look like a tasty treat to me...

Step 1

Tie a piece of string to the top of a pinecone.

Step 2

Smother the pinecone in peanut butter, using a spoon. Then roll it in birdseed and hang it up in the garden.

If your bird feeder starts to look old or get moldy, recycle it and make a nice new one!

Step 3

Get an adult to help you prepare some plain popcorn, then use a needle and thread to join about 50 pieces of popcorn together. Hang it up outside. The birds will love it!

HOW DOES IT WORK?

If you hang your feeders within view of your window, you can observe the birds from indoors so they aren't disturbed. A lot of people put feeders out to help the birds make it through the cold winter, when it can be hard for birds to find food. Watch carefully and see if you can identify different species. See how they interact with each other. Is there a pecking order?

Plain popcorn is very healthy, as well as delicious.

DNA FROM STRAWBERRIES

DNA is the thing that makes you YOU. It is found in every one of your cells, and contains the instructions that your body has followed to make you the way you are. Every living creature has different DNA. Now you can see the DNA of strawberries in your own kitchen!

YOU WILL NEED:

★ A freezer

★ 3 strawberries and salt

★ A measuring cup

★ Scissors

★ A paper kitchen towel

★ A plastic bag

★ 2 plastic cups

★ Laundry detergent (liquid or powdered)

★ A glass

★ Ice cubes

★ 2 big bowls

★ A fork and a teaspoon

★ A toothpick

★ Ice-cold rubbing alcohol (ask an adult for help)

Step 1

Put the rubbing alcohol in the freezer at least an hour before you do this experiment.

Step 2

Remove the stems from the strawberries and break them up using a fork.

Step 3

Put the pieces into a measuring cup. Add one teaspoon of detergent to half a cup of warm water and pour the mixture over the fruit.

Step 4

Stand the cup in a bowl of warm water. The detergent and warm water will start breaking up the strawberry cells. Wait 12 minutes, stirring often.

Step 5

Next, stand the cup in a bowl of ice cubes for 5 minutes.

Want some strawberry DNA with that?

Step 6

Cut the corner off the plastic bag and line it with the paper towel. Then pour the strawberry mush through so the liquid containing the DNA collects in a cup.

Step 7

Add a quarter teaspoon of salt to the collected liquid and mix it well.

Step 8

Now pour some of the mixture into a clear glass, so it is about a third full. Ask an adult to pour in an equal amount of ice-cold rubbing alcohol, and then rock the glass gently.

Step 9

Let the glass stand for a few minutes. A cloudy patch should form at the top of the mixture. It may look bubbly or whiteish. This is strawberry DNA! You can remove it with a toothpick. It will look like clear slime! Isn't it incredible to think that the slime contains all the information for making a strawberry plant?

HOW DOES IT WORK?

To get to a strawberry's DNA, first we mash the fruit to break open its cells. Then we separate the cells into their parts, using the enzymes in washing detergent. The ice stops the detergent from breaking apart the DNA itself. Then we filter the mixture, and the liquid we are left with is called the "supernatent," which contains the DNA. Finally, adding salt and rubbing alcohol makes the DNA break apart from the rest of the solution and rise to the top.

BUG HUNTERS

Time to get up close to some creepy crawlies! They might not be the most pleasant of creatures, but these little guys are a very important part of nature.

There are hundreds of insects under our feet!

Step 1

Find a flat area of ground where you have permission to dig. Make a hole with a trowel, deep enough to hold a your glass jar upright.

Step 2

Put some grass and leaves in the hole.

Step 3

Place the jar in the hole without a lid, standing upright to make a trap.

Step 4

Cover the trap with grass and leaves.

Step 5

Protect the trap from the rain by covering the hole with with a glass or plastic lid.

Step 6

Check your trap the following day to see what's in it!

Step 7

Can you identify the bugs and creepy crawlies? Check on the web or in your library, to find the names and habits of these creatures.

HOW DOES IT WORK?

When bugs fall into your trap, they find it hard to climb back out again because the glass sides are so smooth. See if you can identify the insects that you have caught. Look at them through a magnifying glass to see them in greater detail. Make sure you return the insects to the outdoors when you have had a good look. Leaving insects in the trap for a long time is cruel and could kill them.

ULTIMATE TASTE TEST

Time to put your taste buds to the test! Can you still taste properly when your sense of smell is cut off?

YOU WILL NEED:

★ An apple

★ A potato

★ A vegetable peeler

★ A chopping board

★ A knife

★ A plate

★ A friend

Step 1

Peel an apple and a potato and cut them in to similar sized pieces. Arrange them in two groups on a plate. Remember which is which!

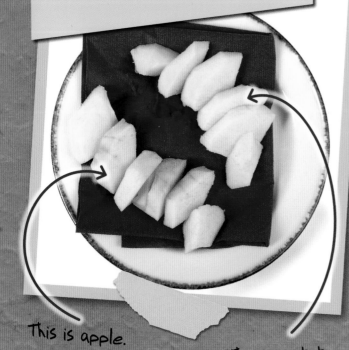

This is apple.

This is potato.

Step 2

Put a blindfold on your friend.

22

Step 3

Get your friend to hold their nose as they taste one piece, then another.

Step 4

Can your friend tell which is which?

I think this experiment is a bit tasteless!

HOW DOES IT WORK?

To work out the flavor of food, we rely on our sense of taste and sense of smell working together. When one of them is cut out, we cannot accurately tell what we are eating.

THIS WAY UP

Plants grow up and their roots go down. But what happens if you start messing with gravity?

YOU WILL NEED:

★ Blotting paper
★ A glass jar
★ A packet of radish or bean seeds
★ A teaspoon
★ Scissors

Step 1

Cut out a piece of blotting paper that fits around the inside of the jar.

Step 2

Put the blotting paper in the jar and add a little water, just enough to make it damp all over.

I wonder what happens if you grow seeds in space?

Step 3

Carefully push radish or bean seeds between the glass and the blotting paper. You may need to use a teaspoon to help with this.

This bit can be tricky!

Step 4

Put the jar on a cool window sill, away from direct sunlight.

Step 5

Check the seeds every day. Keep the blotting paper damp.

The roots grow downward.

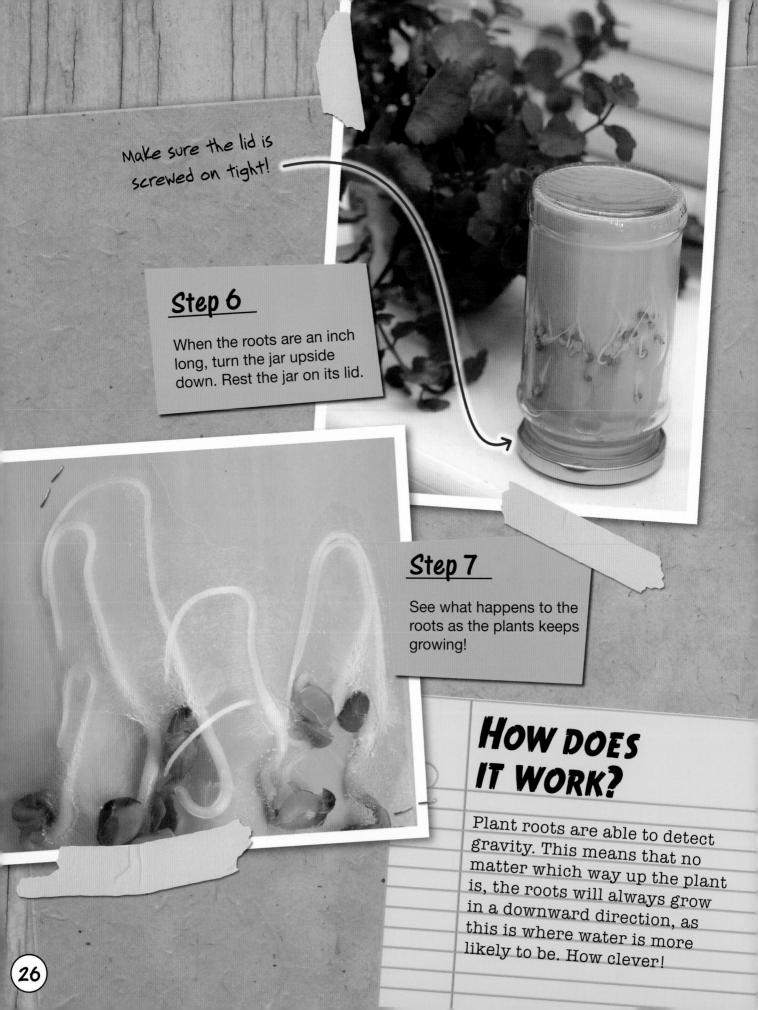

Make sure the lid is screwed on tight!

Step 6

When the roots are an inch long, turn the jar upside down. Rest the jar on its lid.

Step 7

See what happens to the roots as the plants keeps growing!

HOW DOES IT WORK?

Plant roots are able to detect gravity. This means that no matter which way up the plant is, the roots will always grow in a downward direction, as this is where water is more likely to be. How clever!

RIGHT VERSUS LEFT

You will know if you are left- or right-handed, but did you know that you can have other body parts that are dominant? Try these simple tests to see!

YOU WILL NEED:

★ A pencil and notebook to record your findings

★ An empty paper towel tube

★ A cup of water

★ A small ball to catch

★ A larger ball to kick

★ A friend

Step 1

Ask a friend to perform some simple exercises. For each one, note down which side of their body they use to do things.

Are you alright, or all left?

Step 2

Ask your friend to wink. Which eye do they use? Make a note.

Step 3

Ask your friend to look through an empty cardboard tube. They should do it first with both eyes open, then close each eye in turn.

Ask them if what they saw changed as they closed either eye. Did they see better with left or right? Write it down.

Step 4

Ask your friend to write something. Then give them a cup. Finally, have them throw a ball. Which hand do they use each time? Make a note.

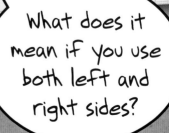

What does it mean if you use both left and right sides?

Step 5

Jumping and kicking tests: ask your friend to jump forward on one leg. Then drop a ball on the floor and ask them to kick it. Which foot do they use each time?

You might be mixed-handed or ambidextrous!

Step 6

Look at your results. Does your friend always use the same side? Which side do they use the most often?

HOW DOES IT WORK?

About 80% of people are right-handed, and 10% of people are left-handed. If you prefer one hand for some tasks and the other for other tasks, you are mixed-handed. If you are equally good with both, that is called ambidextrous! Scientists are not sure why most people tend to favor their right sides.

GLOSSARY

ambidextrous
(am-bih-DEK-strus)
Able to use either
the right or left hand
with equal strength
and control.

calcium
(KAL-see-um) A silvery
white metallic element
that is an important part
of plants and animals.

capacity
(kuh-PA-sih-tee) The
amount that something
can hold.

DNA
(dee-en-AY) A
complicted chain of
chemicals inside each
cell, giving each
organisim its special
qualities.

element
(EH-luh-ment) A
substance, such as iron
or oxygen, that cannot
be broken down into
other substances using
ordinary chemical
processes.

enzyme (EN-zym)
A chemical that speeds
up the way in which
substances react with
each other.

microorganism
(my-kroh-OR-guh-
nih-zum) A living creature
that is too small for us to
see with the naked eye.

nectar (NEK-tur)
A sweet liquid produced
by plants; bees and
other insects are
attracted by nectar.

pollen (PAH-lin)
A mass of dustlike
particles that flowers
produce when they
reproduce.

predator (PREH-duh-ter)
An animal that attacks
and eats other animals.

react (ree-AKT)
To change after coming
into contact with another
substance.

solution
(suh-LOO-shun) A liquid
in which something has
been dissolved; sugar
dissolves in coffee to
make a solution.

waggle (WA-gul)
To sway or move from
side to side.

xylem (ZY-lum)
Plant cells that contain
tubes to help the plant
draw water and other
materials upward.

Searching
glossary
database...

FURTHER READING

Albert, Toni. ***Busy With Bugs: 160 Extremely Interesting Things to Do With Bugs***. Mechanicsburg, PA: Trickle Creek Books, 2011.

Ballard, Carol. ***How Your Mouth and Nose Work***. New York: Gareth Stevens Publishing, 2011.

Chahrour, Janet Parks. ***Zap! Blink! Taste! Think!: Exciting Life Science for Curious Minds***. Hauppauge, NY: Barron's Educational Series, 2003.

Doudna, Kelly. ***Super Simple Things to Do With Plants: Fun and Easy Science for Kids***. Minneapolis, MN: Super SandCastle, 2011.

Einspruch, Andrew. ***DNA Detectives***. New York: PowerKids Press: 2013.

Pollan, Michael. ***The Omnivore's Dilemma for Kids: The Secrets Behind What You Eat.*** New York: Dial Books for Younger Readers, 2010.

VanCleave, Janice Pratt. ***Step-by-Step Science Experiments in Biology***. New York: Rosen Central, 2013.

Websites

For web resources related to the subject of this book, go to: www.windmillbooks.com/weblinks and select this book's title.

INDEX

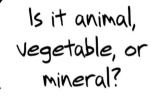

Is it animal, vegetable, or mineral?

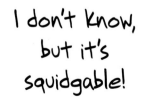

I don't know, but it's squidgable!

Miss Smith
Under the Ocean

SCHOOL BUS

MICHAEL GARLAND

SCHOLASTIC INC.

ISBN 978-0-545-53939-5

12 11 10 9 8 7 6 5 4 3 2 1   13 14 15 16 17 18/0

Printed in the U.S.A.   08

This edition first printing, January 2013

Designed by Jason Henry

To all the fish in the sea

"Well, class, I hope you all enjoy today's trip to the aquarium," Miss Smith said to her students after they got off the bus at their destination.

"Much of the earth is covered by water, and it is home to all kinds of plant and animal life. Today we are going to read from some wonderful stories that take place on the high seas," said Miss Smith, opening her book and starting to read.

Zack really loved hearing his teacher, Miss Smith, read from her *Incredible Storybook*. Whenever she read from the book, the stories actually came alive.

Miss Smith's first words were . . . "The Owl and the Pussycat went to sea in a beautiful pea-green boat . . . "

In an instant, Miss Smith and the whole class were crowded into the little green boat with the Owl and the Pussycat, bobbing up and down in the waves, far from any shore.

The Owl and the Pussycat looked surprised to see so many people with them. But Miss Smith didn't miss a beat! She opened her book and started to read again, but this time she read from *Moby Dick*. Just then, a huge white whale lunged out of the water and splashed down next to their boat, nearly capsizing them.

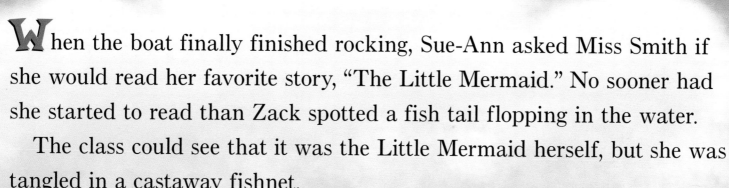

When the boat finally finished rocking, Sue-Ann asked Miss Smith if she would read her favorite story, "The Little Mermaid." No sooner had she started to read than Zack spotted a fish tail flopping in the water.

The class could see that it was the Little Mermaid herself, but she was tangled in a castaway fishnet.

"We have to save her!" shouted Zack.

The Pussycat quickly steered the pea-green boat to one side of the twisted net, then some of the class reached over and grabbed it so the Little Mermaid could get free.

"Oh, thank you," said the mermaid, after she was pulled up into the boat.
"You're just in time for a story," Miss Smith said to the Little Mermaid.
"Oh, goodie, I love pirate tales!" answered the mermaid.
Miss Smith started to read *Treasure Island* and sure enough, a short distance away everyone saw a pirate ship. It was stranded high and dry on a big rock that stuck out of the water.

The little green boat carefully approached the grounded ship.

"Ahoy there! Anybody home?" shouted Miss Smith.

"Ahoy yourself! We're home all right. And we're stuck, too," said Captain Long John Silver as he leaned over the rail with the rest of his cranky crew of pirates.

"Can we help?" Zack asked.

Long John Silver replied. "Yes, you can. We were searching for the island where we buried our treasure, when we ran aground. Can you mateys give us a ride?"

Without even waiting for an answer, the pirates climbed down from their
ship and squeezed into the pea-green boat.

"There's an island close by," said the Little Mermaid. "Maybe that's where you buried your treasure." So they headed there while Derrick took the book and started to read from a story called *Robinson Crusoe*.

When they reached the beach, a very happy man dressed in ragged clothes greeted them.

"Am I glad to see you!" said Robinson Crusoe. "I've been shipwrecked here so long. It's very lonely!"

"Would you like to hear a story, Mr. Crusoe?"

"Would I ever!" he said.

Zack took the book and chose a story called *Gulliver's Travels*. As soon as he started reading, they could all hear a faint voice being carried by the wind.

"Help me! Help me!"

The voice was coming from a sailor named Gulliver. He was tied down to the ground by an army of tiny people called Lilliputians.

"Shoo, shoo," said Miss Smith. The Lilliputians scattered, and Miss Smith and her class helped untie the man.

"Thank you very much," said Gulliver. Then they noticed that the wind was picking up and blowing dark storms in their direction.

What to do now? Miss Smith thought. *I know!*

She picked up her *Incredible Storybook* and started reading a story called *Twenty Thousand Leagues Under the Sea*. The next moment the *Nautilus* submarine appeared by the shore.

The hatch opened, and Captain Nemo popped out.

"Can I be of assistance?" he asked. His voice could barely be heard above the roaring wind.

"Yes, a short trip in your submarine would be wonderful right now," Miss Smith shouted back.

"By all means! Welcome aboard," said Captain Nemo with a wave of his cap.

Once everyone was safely aboard, the *Nautilus* disappeared below the crashing waves into a quiet undersea world.

The submarine glided through the deep blue water. The view from the portholes was spectacular. Everywhere the class looked there were strange and colorful fish.

Captain Nemo gave a tour and explained everything they were seeing. "The *Nautilus* was built to study the world under the oceans and let people know how important it is to the earth." Just then, the *Nautilus* began to shake violently.

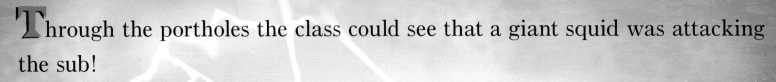

Through the portholes the class could see that a giant squid was attacking the sub!

It wrapped its tentacles around the *Nautilus* and lifted it right out of the water! It seemed as though the submarine would snap like a pretzel.

"Somebody *do* something!" screeched Sue-Ann.

"Full speed ahead!" said Zack, tugging Nemo's sleeve.

Captain Nemo cranked up the engines until they roared. The submarine could only inch forward, but the giant squid held on tight. Everyone closed their eyes—then finally, the giant squid lost its grip, and the sub shot up through the water. They were safe!

When the *Nautilus* surfaced, the storm was over, and the sun was setting. Miss Smith, the class, and the whole cast of storybook characters assembled on top.

"Well, it's been quite an exciting day, but it's getting late," said Miss Smith.
Then she finished reading the end of each story so all the characters could
go back into the *Incredible Storybook*. When she read the very last word,
quick as a flash, the class was back at the aquarium, heading for the bus.
Zack thought to himself, *I'll never look at the ocean the same way again.*